My first poem that I can remember writing is the poem I wrote when I was 16 years old to my childhood sweetheart, Traci. She is now my wife, and we have been married 26 years! Through the years I have written several poems to her, but I think my first one is still one of my favorites:

I love you more than I can say
For there could never be a way
To put in words, so oft unclear
The way I feel toward you, my dear!

I love you more than can be told
I treasure you above pure gold
You are to me, of priceless worth
More dear to me than all the Earth

Of all the lovely sights there are,
A crimson rose, a shooting star,
A butterfly, or fawn and doe
You are the loveliest sight I know!

Were I to search the whole world through
I'd find no other quite like you
Someone so sweet in every way
I love you more than I can say!

I think we have all faced the challenge of dieting. We may have good intentions and high motivations, but it just is not a very easy thing to do. Maybe it is no coincidence that "diet" starts with "die" because it seems that saying "no" to the foods we like will just about kill us. Well, here's a poem that reflects the challenge of dieting:

The Diet Plan

I thought I would go on a diet,
But my stomach just wouldn't keep quiet.
My tummy would growl,
With a blood-curling howl,
For the hunger was causing a riot.

So I switched to the diet called Atkins,
And I set all the food out on napkins;
The meat, eggs and cheese.
Just as much as you please;
But I cheated with too many "snack-ins."

Oh the seafood diet came next,
And I found myself feeling perplexed,
For I ate with such glee,
All the food I could see,
What else would you really expect?

All diets I now have forsaken.
A bold, new course I have taken.
To avoid all the sorrow,
Don't weigh 'til tomorrow.
Dear friend, would you please pass the bacon?

Sometimes it is hard to know if a need is legitimate of if someone is trying to "pull one over on you." As a pastor I've received a lot of calls from a lot of people. I wish I could help everyone. I don't want to take the Lord's money and pass it on to someone who is not being honest about their situation.

Many years ago I received a call from an elderly lady asking if I would give her a ride to the Emergency Room. I asked her what had happened and she told me she had stubbed her toe. I asked her if anyone else in her house might be able to give her a ride. She said, "No, they are all watching the Academy Awards on TV, and so I couldn't possibly ask them to take me!"

I sit in my office and study a book
I hear someone knocking and so take a look
I see in my doorway a man that seems shook
So I wonder if he is legit or a crook

He tells me how sadly he's down on his luck
And he's trying to get me to lend him a buck
For food in his belly and gas in his truck
He sounds so sincere that I really feel stuck

For if this could be a legitimate need
I'm all about helping the hungry to feed
But if he's a scoundrel with motive of greed
I don't want his mission of theft to succeed

I've heard all the stories of grief and of woe
Of homes that were lost and there's nowhere to go
Of checks in the mail but the postman is slow
Of money that's needed for someone's stubbed toe

I want to be careful, for this is my fear
I'd hate to give cash which they'd use to buy beer
But I also would wish that I'd never appear
To hold back assistance when needs are so clear

So may the Lord grant me His wisdom and grace
May He give discernment to handle each case
Pease grant special insight for running life's race
May I hear "well done" when I see His dear face!

Some time back, my youngest son was playing hide and seek at church and ended up breaking through some drywall. He didn't get hurt, and so I wrote a poem:

For me, as a Pastor
'Twas quite a disaster
When my son
Made a run
Right through the plaster

My anger containing
I asked for explaining
So he said
(With face red)
"My sister was gaining"

With tools I am wielding
It's time for rebuilding
May I see
It will be
A wall that's unyielding

Maybe just about everyone has a beloved relative that loves to cook and loves to see people enjoy the food. This poem is in honor of all the grandmas and other dear loved ones who make an art of cooking, and who make a eating contest out of every meal.

Whenever we traveled to see my Aunt Betty
She always would serve us big plates of spaghetti
With plenty of noodles and meatballs and sauce
All dieting plans would meet total loss.

My brother's bad manners were total disgrace
Oregano sauce would cover his face
It's tough to eat noodles without ever slurping
And tougher to get them all down without burping.

We'd eat 'til our stomachs were feeling quite sore
Aunt Betty insisted we always take more
She gave us more sauce; she gave us more noodles
No matter we said, "We've already had oodles!"

Her cooking established a happy tradition
I'm thinking Aunt Betty deserves recognition
Let's have a parade and let's throw some confetti
For lovely Aunt Betty, the Queen of Spaghetti!

This next poem could have been written by Pastor Blackstone of the Bunny In The Hat Baptist Church,

Oh pulpit committee, I think you should search,
And find a magician to pastor your church.
A man who has mastered the ministry trick
Of study, and visits, and blessing the sick.

Not rabbits, but sermons he pulls from his hat,
And leaves people saying, "Now, how'd he do that?"
Whenever he preaches the truth loud and clear
Some folks will just magically soon disappear.

He keeps visitation cards tucked up his sleeve.
He knows when to enter and knows when to leave.
He makes people cry and he makes people laugh.
He really would like to saw Deacons in half.

They think he can magically know every name,
And treat every member exactly the same.
So when the whole matter is all said and done,
A Master Magician, he HAS to be one!

Let's face it – we men just do not like to go to the doctor. We don't want them to find anything wrong with us, and we don't want to admit we need any help.

Each year at the Southern Baptist Convention there is a free health screening available. One year I was diagnosed with high sugar. My wife thought I should go to the doctor, but I made a deal with her. I would eat oatmeal every day for a year, and then at the next Convention's health screening, if my sugar count was still above 100, I would go see a doctor. After a year of daily oatmeal breakfasts, I had my sugar checked and it was 97. A deal is a deal. I avoided the visit to the doctor. I would rather eat oatmeal for a whole year than go see a doctor one time.

Makes sense to me.

My wife told me clearly in words firm and strong,
You've put off your doctor appointment too long!
You know you are hurting, you know you are sick,
The doctor can help you to feel better quick!

My answer to her was a thoughtful reply,
Responding just like any other tough guy
Now why should I go and get medicine for it?
My problem will pass, if I just will ignore it!

Physicians are not any smarter than me
Who cares if they do have a doctor's degree?
Just give me my pillow, my blanket, and couch
Ignore me for acting a bit like a grouch!

The doctor could give me some pills of my own
But I'd rather just lie on the sofa and moan
When we've all had enough of this pain & this sorrow
I'll give in and go, but let's wait 'til tomorrow!

We recently held an Ordination Service at our church, and it brought back lots of memories of my own Ordination. It can be a bit stressful to anticipate all the deep, theological questions that may get asked. Here's a poem to commemorate the occasion:

Ordination Service

Remember your ordination service?
Were you feeling a little bit nervous?
Were you dreading the difficult questions?
And braced for some pointed suggestions?

And at your ordination did you feel temptation
To use the occasion to give an oration
On how your vocation would lead to salvation
Of souls in damnation and bring transformation
To those in stagnation so your congregation
Would feel great elation and much celebration?

Ordinations must be the best place
To discuss the deep issues of Grace
And settle great doctrines of life
Such as -- where did Cain get his wife?

I really don't get upset when people fall asleep during a sermon. I know that there can be many reasons: medication, work schedules, or maybe my sermon is just not that interesting to them. The one thing that gets to me a little bit is – when I see someone sleep the entire sermon, and then they come up to me afterwards and say, "Pastor, what a wonderful sermon you just preached!"

There once was a Reverend McDurman
Longwinded when preaching a sermon
Church members declare
They're nodding in prayer
Not sleeping, as some might determine

Another fact about a lot of us men is that we pride ourselves on our ability to cook meat. Many of us believe we are experts and many of us have heavily guarded secrets to our success. Thank you to all the women out there who let us think we are pretty good at it. And thank you also to whoever invented the microwave. After I cook the meat long enough for my taste, my wife usually needs to give it a little more help.

I truly hope to someday hear the Lord say "Well done, thou good and faithful servant." But if anyone asks me how I want my steak, the answer is "Medium rare, thou good and faithful chef!"

The Grill

How noble the man who can master the grill
His powers allow us our bellies to fill
With skillful precision he summons the fires
Arranges the meat as perfection requires
Cooks never too little and never too much
But always the perfect and delicate touch
That brings to our taste buds a glorious thrill
Our hero, our victor, the King of the Grill!

Some time ago I heard someone mention a few words for which there is no rhyme: purple, silver, month, and orange. I kind of took that as a challenge, and came up with a poem that used those words. Now, you have to read it just right, and give it a little help, but with some "poetic license" I think we've done it!

Words That Don't Rhyme

I knew a girl who spent her time
In search of words which have no rhyme
She finally got it through her skull
There's just no way to rhyme "purple"

An English teacher joined the task
But found it far too much to ask
For meditative thoughts will blur
To rhyme a word with this - "silver"

Another friend spoke with a lisp
He never could talk clear and crisp
But he would practith every month
To find a non-rhyme word just onth!

A genius received the call
To rhyme the hardest word of all
He could not rhyme a word with "orange"
'til he bumped his head upon the door hinge!

Some holidays make a lot more sense than others. For instance, it's wonderful to celebrate Christmas, Easter, and Thanksgiving. But why do we celebrate April Fool's Day? I just don't have an answer for that. But I do have a poem for it:

April Fools

So, who invented April Fools?
And who's the guy that wrote the rules?
And who came up with pulling pranks?
I'd like to know, to give my thanks!

For all the times some cunning stinker
Made me take hook, line, and sinker
And thanks for all the times I bit
And fell for someone's clever wit!

You've had your laughs, you've had your fun
You think you're such a crafty one
You've likely planned your next attack,
Enjoy the day, but watch your back!

To all the Boy Scouts out there, my compliments on
your ability to tie all the complicated knots. It amazes
me that knots have names like "Granny" or "Sheet
bend" or "Clove hitch." I am not too great in the knot
tying area of life, so I thought I would try to write a
poem without getting my tongue tied –

Boy Scout Knot

I tried to tie a Boy Scout knot
I thought I could, but I could not
I used to know, but I forgot
I even gave it my best shot
I really tried, and tried a lot
I tried 'til I was tired and hot
Alas for me, 'twas all for naught
The knot was bad -- a naughty knot!

I have no idea where the phrase "Monkey On My Back" came from, but I know is can be a struggle for a lot of people. If we have a reputation to live up to, or shoes to fill of someone who simply cannot be replaced, or some kind of a jinx we just cannot shake. To anyone who is facing that challenge, I wish you freedom, blessings and a fresh start!

Monkey On My Back

It sure is hard to stay on track
When there's a monkey on your back
And all the while he stays up there
You know some folks will point and stare!

A monkey may look sweet and cute
But he deserves to get the boot
When into all our best intentions
He ever throws his monkey wrenches!

So may I learn to clear the air
And get the monkey down from there
Refresh my mind and set me free
Don't make a monkey out of me!

What is the perfect length of time for a sermon? I always hope to quit preaching just before the congregation quits listening. I heard someone say once that if you're preaching, and you haven't struck oil in 30 minutes, it's time to stop boring!

How Long A Sermon?

If I had the courage, then here's what I'd do
I'd question church members who sit in the pew
And ask them to honestly answer for me
Exactly how lengthy a sermon should be?

Perhaps they would say thirty minutes is plenty
But truly they'd rather say closer to twenty
And if you are planning to preach about sin
You might better whittle it down to just ten

But then, there are some who will say to go longer
To show to the world they are spiritually stronger
The longer you're preaching the more they are blest
They're nodding in prayer, or getting their rest?

All of God's children ought to be praising Him! Praise is such a powerful force! We ought to remind ourselves that praise is the opposite of complaining, and God hates complaining. It was the grumbling of the Old Testament Israelites that brought on the fiery serpents. On the other hand, if we will show the Lord we are eager to praise Him, He just might give us even more reasons to be praising Him. Here's a poem about praise:

Praise

When it's praise that we raise,
We lift haze from our days.
When it's doom we assume,
We bring gloom to the room.
So give cheer, far and near,
Make it clear, why we're here.
With a word, hearts are stirred,
Be assured, praise is heard.

Have you ever witnessed a true, life-changing Revival? Remember II Chronicles 7:14, and let's always be praying for a touch from Heaven!

Revival

When sermons are preached,
And people are reached
When children are brought,
And lessons are taught
When Bibles are read,
And praises are said
When lost souls are found,
And blessings abound
When old wounds are healed,
And God's plan revealed
When prayer needs are met,
And Satan's upset
When church songs inspire,
And hearts are on fire
Then the Church is alive,
And God's people will thrive!

Recently, a fine young man in our church became an Eagle Scout. It was my privilege to have a part in the service in which he became an Eagle Scout, and I was honored to contribute a poem to the occasion:

The Eagle Scout

Today we honor a fine young man,
For reaching the goal, fulfilling the plan.
What morals and ethics are all about,
To carry the title of Eagle Scout!

He seeks the path of adventure and thrills,
For he's well-equipped with survival skills.
He keeps his calm when others are scared,
For his motto is always be prepared.

He loves to be in the great outdoors,
As each new pathway he explores;
Rappelling and rafting and pitching a tent,
Hunting and fishing - that's time well spent!

A loyal friend, respectful and kind;
Helping the weary who's fallen behind;
Going beyond what others expect;
Honoring God with fervent respect.

If more young men would follow this pace,
Our nation would be a better place.
The hope for our future is found in our youth,
To walk the path of justice and truth!

That's why we pause to give honor today,
To someone headed the proper way.
A fine young man, without a doubt,
Who has just become an Eagle Scout!

One year for school, my children were selling candy bars for a fund raiser. One lady told them she could not buy a candy bar because she had given up chocolate for Lent. I began to wonder how many different things people had given up for Lent, and then my mind wondered to a silly possibility. Please understand, I mean no disrespect to all who participate in the Lent season. I just happened to think of an amusing choice and came up with this poem:

Lint For Lent

For much of my life there has been an event
Of many glad hours I've happily spent
I go to the dryer and open the vent
To practice my hobby – collecting the lint

It makes me so happy, one hundred percent
To scoop it and roll it, I'm one happy gent
It's warm and it's fuzzy, it has a fresh scent
Three cheers for the treasure and value of lint!

But then I consider with bitter lament
That Easter is coming, it's time to repent
Resolved and determined, I must not relent
I'll sacrifice something in honor of lent

I've chosen, albeit my heart will be rent
I'll summon my courage and give my consent
To chasten my soul to the furthest extent
This season of lent, I am giving up lint!

A church is a wonderful place to enjoy a fellowship supper! There are many delicious servings of food provided by such wonderful cooks! One day, it struck me that if you had a casserole of meat, and added okra to it, you could have a funny result. It would be "meaty-okra" or "mediocre" so, of course, a poem was soon to follow:

Church casserole

'Twas a cook who could be quite a joker,
Eat his food and you might be a choker,
But to give some relief
He mixed okra and beef,
Not great, not bad, mediocre!

Now this next poem is one that I'm scared to include. It's going to be hard for it not to be taken the wrong way. I just ask you to understand it is totally "tongue-in-cheek" and not to be taken seriously at all. I was told once that I was a humble person. It just kind of struck me funny that I should be careful not to be proud of being told that I was humble. Then, the next step was to write a poem about being proud of being humble, and so here's the result:

I'm Humble

Oh say, don't you wish you were humble like me?
The thing I most proud of, is humility!
I'm smart as an ox, and strong as a geek,
But I am not haughty, instead I am meek.

I must be good looking, 'cause folks always say,
They're wanting my picture, to keep bugs away.
I'm quick as a tack, and sharp on my feet,
But humble and gracious, toward all who I meet.

I possess hidden talent, and friends always tell
How impressive it is that I hide it so well!
I'm the humblest person you ever will see.
I bet that you wish you were humble like me!

Our church has a Trio comprised of me as Pastor, and two staff members. I greatly enjoy singing with the other two men. In fact, I told the church the name of our Trio could be Psalm 23 because it's "Thy Ron and thy staff." (It would have been even better if my name was Rodney instead of Ronald)

Usually, things work out just fine, but one Sunday we somehow got off, and just couldn't find our way back. So I wrote a poem to the church about our Trio calamity:

Church Trio

Oh me, oh my, oh mio!
I tried to sing in a trio,
But then we got off key-o,
And it really hurt my ego!

First slower, and then faster,
But the tempo could not master.
For the staff and this poor Pastor,
It ended in disaster!

My ears remain a ringing
With our failed attempt at singing
My heart is still a stinging
From the notes that we were slinging

If you don't succeed at first
Try again to quench your thirst
Don't believe that you've been cursed
Mistakes must be reversed

We will give it another go!
Resilience we must show!
To new heights we will grow!
Just me, and Curly, and Mo!

When there is snow in the forecast, the children in our church get very excited. They get almost as excited as the Teachers in our church.

In the Book of Job, in the King James Bible, there is a phrase "The treasures of the snow." That's a phrase that's just begging to have a poem written about it:

Treasures Of The Snow

The Book of Job records the phrase,
"The treasures of the snow."
I wonder what the value is,
He spoke of long ago?

Say, could it be the snowball fights
Between two snow-walled forts?
Or maybe it's vacation plans
To visit ski resorts?

Perhaps he meant the joy that's felt
To watch a child so young,
Who makes his first attempt to catch
A snowflake on his tongue.

From making snowy angel shapes,
To backyard ice skate rinks.
From building snowmen six feet tall,
To fresh hot cocoa drinks.

There's lots of games and things to do
Before the snowfall ends.
And many special times to spend
With family and friends.

The greatest treasure of the snow
Must be, without a doubt,
To spread the word to young and old
The news that school is out!

While we're on the topic of snow, here's a poem about the tiny size hole in the frosted windshield that many of us men scrape out to see through:

Ice Scraper

I put on my coat, and walked out to the car;
Then quickly I noticed I wouldn't get far.
The windshield was covered completely with frost,
But my schedule was busy, no time to be lost!
I got out the scraper, the chiseling began;
And I did my duty, like any true man.
I scratched out an opening two inches square.
That's all that is needed with plenty to spare!
No reason to worry, I'm safe as can be!
I'm driving by instinct, I don't need to see!
I'm confident, ready, and in full control,
For all that I need is my tiny peep hole!

A lady in our church asked me where in the Bible is the verse that talks about God keeping record of our tears. Her husband was a treasured, long-time member of our church, but was nearing the time of his passage to Heaven. I found the verse and wrote this poem in his honor:

(Psalm 56:8 & Revelation 21:4)

The Last Tear

From time to time, the trials of life
Bring sorrow to the heart.
There's sickness, pain, and loneliness;
Dear friends with whom we part.

And with the grief, there comes the tears
We oft' try to conceal.
The telltale signs of brokenness
Expressing how we feel.

But God's dear Word declares each tear
Is noticed by our Lord.
And every tear that's ever shed
He promised to record.

But there will come a glorious day
Up there beyond the skies,
When God will wipe the tears away
From all His children's eyes!

Then no more sadness, only joy:
No mourning, only peace.
Just happy hearts all filled with love;
The sorrows all will cease.

The final tear will someday fall,
And no more sadness then.
For when the last tear's wiped away,
The praise will just begin!

Our family went to Pigeon Forge, TN and toured the Titanic exhibit. We were very impressed, and I got an idea for a poem about it:

Sail With God
It must have been frantic, to sail the Titanic
With iceburgs drifting about.
The hole thru the hull, sent howls through the halls;
It was scary for them, there's no doubt.

What led to the gloom? What brought on the doom?
And what pushed them over the brink?
Place the blame & the shame on those with the claim,
"There's a ship even God cannot sink."

From Noah we know, for the Scriptures do show
God is able to keep ships afloat.
We will only endure, and be truly secure
With the presence of God in our boat!

Serving on a Committee can be a long, time-consuming process. If you have ever served on a Church Committee, you probably can relate to this next poem:

On The Committee

I beg you have mercy upon me, take pity!
I'm currently serving upon a committee.
A Baptist committee assembling a horse
Will make it turn out like a camel, of course!
We sit still for hours while making our motions.
Our minutes we write to take note of our notions.
The Rules of dear Robert we faithfully quote,
To keep us in order each time that we vote.
So, here's to the joy of eternal discussions,
And all of the questions and all repercussions.
The most precious phrase in the world I have learned
Is the simple expression - "The meeting's adjourned!"

Each April 15th, we face the challenge of filing our Income Taxes. Back in Bible times, there seemed to be a different way to take care of the taxes. I sure do wish we could go back to the way Jesus took care of it in His day!

Paying Taxes

A man came to Peter to find out the facts,
Is Jesus intending on paying the tax?
So Peter asked Jesus just what they would do;
The answer was quite a surprise to him too!

For Jesus told Peter to go get a hook,
Then bait it and cast it into a near brook.
The first fish you catch, just look in its gills;
There's a coin you can use to pay our tax bills!

So now when the fifteenth of April comes 'round,
And all of the taxes add up and abound,
To solve all my problems, I truly am wishing
What I really should do, is just go fishing!

Sometimes, during a sermon, there can be a lot of distractions. The challenge is to keep right on preaching in spite of them. Here's a poem about a worst-case scenario of sermon distractions:

Sermon Time

I walked to the pulpit all ready for preaching,
When all of a sudden I heard such a screeching,
I saw in the back of the church was a mother
Holding one child while scolding another!

'Twas kicking and yelling and screaming and fighting,
With slapping and poking and spitting and biting.
And right at that moment, to add to the fray
A church mouse decided to come out and play!

And quicker than I could scarce take in a breath,
Some hymnals went flying, they stoned it to death!
So just when I figured things couldn't get worse,
A dear saintly lady reached deep in her purse,

And pulled out a can of pepper spray mace,
And made sure the rodent had run its last race.
From fist-fighting families, to death spray on vermin,
Oh how in the world could I get through my sermon?

I paused for a moment, all my courage to rally,
And delivered my sermon There's Peace in the Valley

Church softball teams are a great resource for those of us who still think of ourselves as athletes. One time, while playing second base, I was struck on the forehead by a batted ball and ended up getting stiches. (Yes, I should have caught the ball, but I didn't) When the doctor came in to do the stitching, he asked how the accident occurred. I told him it was church softball. He replied, "Isn't there supposed to be divine protection against this sort of thing in church softball? At that point, I determined not to tell him I was the Pastor, lest I truly shake his faith!

I'm An Athlete?

I thought I was an athlete,
I felt so big and strong,
Until a bigger stronger fellow
Had to prove me wrong.
I thought that I could throw a ball
Almost out of sight,
Until I saw it land quite near,
Though flung with all my might.
I thought that I could run so fast,
Almost outrun the wind,
Until I felt so winded that
My sprinting had to end.
I thought that I could flex my arms
And prove I am the best,
Until I flexed and held the pose
But no one was impressed.
I thought that I could shoot the ball
And score on every try,
Until I shot and found someone
had raised the goal too high.
I thought I was an athlete,
My dreams have gone "kaput,"
My only sportsman claim for now
Is just my athlete's foot!

Time change is always a challenge. Does anyone really know why we still do it?

Time Change

Can someone please explain to me,
In this great land of brave and free,
Just why we always change our clocks,
And put ourselves through all these shocks?
We're always falling back each fall,
Then after not much time at all,
We spring ahead when spring comes 'round,
Why can't we stay on common ground?
It's daybreak early, light comes soon,
But quickly dark in the afternoon.
My eating times are all confused,
And sleeping schedules all abused.
So many things we must adjust,
It feels me with so much disgust.
There's more complaints I'd put in rhyme,
But I changed my clock and I'm out of time!

Do you get tired of cell phones going off at the wrong time?

Cell Phones

Their phones go off at awkward times,
And loudly play those silly chimes.
To pay for their such selfish crimes,
Let's make them eat a crate of limes.
Oh, those who leave their cell phones on!

A wedding service, soft and still,
A movie, at suspenseful thrill,
A coach's talk to boost team skill,
Yes, all of these, the mood they kill.
Oh, those who leave their cell phones on!

We need to ask some clever chap,
To please invent a cell phone app,
That would produce a voltage zap,
And give their wrist a well-earned slap.
Oh, those who leave their cell phones on!

Not in the church where I Pastor, but I've heard of
other churches having members who actually gossip.
Of course, I cannot write this poem from personal
experience, but I can just imagine from what I've
heard other Pastors talk about:

The Church Gossip

Each church congregation is sure to include,
A dear saintly lady, so sweet and yet shrewd.
She takes heartfelt interest in everyone's life,
But radiates joy when she learns of new strife.
She knows how to whisper, to pry, and to snoop.
She's always the source of the hottest new scoop.
With a smile on her lips, and a gleam in her eye,
The stories she knows are an endless supply.
When everyone's sworn all their silence to keep,
The intimate knowledge that's buried down deep,
The close guarded secrets they'd never expose,
Don't ask how she learns it, but somehow she knows!
So, since we can't stop her, let's use her instead,
When there's announcements that need to be spread,
The way to inform all the folks on the roll,
Is give her the news and say, "Don't tell a soul!"

Here's a poem about hypocrisy:

The Pot And The Kettle

There once was a Pot and a Kettle,
With a score they were trying to settle.
They each answered back,
So, why call me "black,"
When we're made of the same color metal?

A truth can be learned from their quarrel,
Which could gain us victorious laurel.
Why condemn your dear brother,
When you're each like the other?
Be humble - now that's a good moral!

Christmas is a wonderful holiday, but it's easy to get so busy with all the plans, we may miss the true enjoyment of the season. There is a story in the 'Bible about Mary and Martha that gives a good description of some or the mad rush at Christmas time:

Have a Mary Christmas!

Mary and Martha had much to do
Neighbors had come, and Jesus too.
Martha was worried about her chores
Washing dishes and sweeping floors
Mary decided to take a seat
Upon the floor at Jesus' feet
Martha grew angry and went berserk
Demanding Mary should help with the work
Jesus stepped in and spoke to the heart
For Mary had chosen the needful part
We can busy ourselves over tasks without end
Neglecting our time with Jesus to spend
We have to remember the number one thing
Is taking the time to worship our King
So try to relax and say "no" to stress
Let's worship much more, and worry much less
Wherever you go and whatever you do
I'm wishing a sweet "Mary Christmas" to you!

Here's a poem to remember:

Memory

I remember a time when my memory was good
My brain cells functioning just as they should
But now that some aging has crept up on me
I've noticed a change from how things used to be

I find when I go to the grocery store
I'm stopping to think "What did I come here for?"
I meet with a friend that I've known for so long
But embarrass myself when I get his name wrong

I plan with my wife to go out on a date
But forgetting the schedule I'm showing up late
There's something of brilliance I started to say
But it flew from by mind at some point 'long the way

They say to remember some valuable thing
Take one of your fingers and tie on a string
I followed advice and the string I did tie
But for all of my life I just can't recall why

To conquer the problem, I'm writing things down
I'll not let poor memory, change me to a clown
With note taking skills I'm a memory wiz
Soon as I can remember just where my list is!

Here's a poem about a politician:

Politician

There once was a proud politician
Who wanted supreme recognition
His mission of ambition
Raised condition of suspicion
So now he must face deposition

My father in law is a great hunter, and I've had the
privilege of going hunting with him several times.
Here's a poem about the experience:

The Deer Hunt

Walking through the forest with a rifle in my hand,
Trying to be silent as I climb up to my stand,
Sitting in the darkness while I wait the sun to rise,
Feeling keen excitement as the day before me lies.

Misty steam arises from each quickened breath I take,
Chilly air surrounds me as the dawn begins to break,
Slowly now the sun begins to grace the eastern sky,
Golden beams upon the leaves that all around me lie.

Waiting ever patiently for any sight or sound,
Trying to detect the slightest movement all around,
Hoping that I'm facing the direction that I should,
Feeling there's a trophy buck so near me in the wood.

Faintly did I hear the gentle rustling of some leaves?
Oh, the sounds my straining ear so readily believes!
There! I know for certain 'twas the snapping of a twig!
Where is it? A buck or doe, how many, and how big?

Moving not a muscle as I hear the sound draw nigh,
Failing to control my breath - steam billows to the sky!
Wondering if my racing heart will stay within my chest!
Knowing 'tis buck fever – this is hunting at its best!

There it is! A mighty buck! 'Twould be a worthy prize!
See the rack, count the points and estimate his size!
Carefully and cautiously I slowly raise my gun,
Take my aim and pray my shot will be a perfect one!

Squeezing on the trigger 'til I hear the shot ring out,
Thinking it was true but also feeling pangs of doubt,
Watching as the deer is dashing wildly thru the brush,
Listening to his thrashing, ever fainter, then a hush.

Did he fall? Where is he now? And can I find his trail?
Should I wait or follow him? What will my hunt avail?
Careful not to make a noise, I ease onto the ground
Trying to suppress my fear the buck may not be found

Straining now to see if there's a spot of blood to trace,
Wiping beads of nervous perspiration from my face,
Bounding with excitement at the droplets I can see,
Flooding with anticipation, the signs are leading me!

There before me, motionless my hunted treasure lies
Careful to assure his death, I gently tap his eyes,
Not a movement I detect, my hunt has met success!
Gratefully, I thank the Lord Who once again did bless!

Hauling out my deer I feel a wonderful delight,
Tasting in imagination venison tonight!
Longing for the next time when I feel so very grand,
Walking through the forest with a rifle in my hand!

This last poem is the one I treasure the most. Back in 1994, Traci and I were expecting our third child, about 5 months into the pregnancy. We were told by the doctors that our baby had such serious health issues, there was zero chance of survival. We asked the Lord to grant a miracle of healing, and we made a commitment that the baby would belong to the Lord. We named the baby Victoria Len Byers, because we were trusting in the Lord for the Victory, and we, like Hannah and Samuel, were promising to Lend our child to the Lord for His will to be done. In His wisdom, God did not choose to heal our baby, and on May 4, 1994, we went through the sorrow of a stillbirth. Soon afterwards, I was contacted by a man whose wife had cancer and was told she did not have long to live. The man had heard about our painful experience and wanted us to come because he said he thought we would understand what they were going through. I was able to share the gospel with the lady, and she prayed with me a prayer of receiving Jesus as Savior. She passed away soon after, and I was asked to preach the funeral. The next Sunday after the funeral, the husband came forward at the invitation, prayed to receive Christ and was baptized. Of course, we can never fully understand why heart-breaking events take place. But in this case, we believe the Lord used what we went through to make it possible for to reach out to others who needed the Lord. When I was in the hospital with Traci, holding our baby, and weeping; I wrote this poem:

I prayed and hoped and dreamed and longed
For you to come and live
Within my home to fully share
The love my heart could give
But then, before I ever said
A fond, "Hello" to you,
Death snatched you from my arms and made
Me bid a sad, "Adieu."
We never strolled along a lane
Of flowers blooming bright
We never gazed up at the sky
And counted stars at night.
We never laughed and ran and played
Beside a babbling brook
We never sat beside a fire,
And read a story book
We never sat and talked of life
As Dads and Daughters should
I never "worried" over you
As only Fathers could
I never watched you learn and grow
To help you on your way.
No "graduation" or "first step"
Or "lovely wedding day."
So many things I'll always wish,
And "what if" if could be
And things I'll never get to know
And never get to see
And now I cannot ask for you
To come to me, it's true;
But God's dear Word has promised me
That I can come to you.

Oh! Yes, we'll stroll along a lane,
A street of purest gold;
And we'll see flowers blooming bright,
Their beauty is untold
Oh! Yes, we'll laugh and run and play
Beside a babbling stream,
The Crystal Stream from God's own throne
"Twill be just like a dream
Oh! Yes, we'll sit and read a Book
We'll read God's precious Word.
Together we'll enjoy the sweetest
Story ever heard
Oh! Yes, we'll sit and talk of life,
Of everlasting life.
And no more worries will we have,
No pain, no tears, no strife.
Oh! Yes, we'll have our special day,
One long, eternal day.
No night will ever come to us
To chase the light away.
Oh! Yes, I'll tell you, "I love you!"
And "You're my special girl!"
As hand -in-hand we walk along
Those lovely Gates of Pearl
Oh Grave, where is thy victory?
Oh Death, where is thy sting?
We have the victory in the Lord!
What peace this truth does bring!
The trumpet sound, the angel shout,
I'm waiting until then.
For now, I lend you to the Lord,
My sweet Victoria Len!

Proof

Made in the USA
Charleston, SC
12 March 2015